7 Lessons
for
HEALING THE HURT
by
Charlie Petrizzo

**This book is dedicated to my parents,
Cono Petrizzo and the late Carolyn Petrizzo,
and to parents of hurting children everywhere
who, just like my parents, never stop believing
that miracles do happen.**

Copyright 2012 by Charlie Petrizzo
Published by Project 2 Heal
Cover art by Shane Amoroson
Production by Episode XI Studios

Printing History
Edition One, January 2012

2

Acknowledgements

To all my family and friends, both new and old, who have been part of telling the story of my healing journey, thank you. You are proof of how blessed I am to have people who care in my life.

It is such a blessing to think that the tragedies that I went through and put my family through have led me to this point. I just pray that in some small way the insights I have gained can help others who go through similar experiences and give them the hope that someday, with the help of God, everything – even the worst things – will come to make sense.

And so it is to God that I give the greatest thanks for everything that has happened to me and the many blessings that have come my way, including this book and the film, *Charlie's Scars*.

- Charlie Petrizzo

TABLE OF CONTENTS

Foreword

At life's tough crossroads, Charlie Petrizzo discovered the intersection of puppies, children and purpose.

In *7 Lessons for Healing the Hurt*, you'll get to know Charlie and the difficult path that led him to that intersection. Now a grown man, the father of two, a loving husband, and the founder of a non-profit that serves hurting children, Charlie was once a hurting child himself. In fact, he almost died twice before he was 20 years old. According to doctors, his chances of survival were slim both times.

Charlie is still around. As a former journalist and writing coach, I had the privilege of meeting him in the early days of his decision to write this book and share his inspiring story. I learned that Charlie's healing journey has been painful, long and ultimately a triumph of the human spirit. His story affected me deeply because of my own painful and life-changing experiences growing up with a younger sister who had a degenerative muscle disorder in an era when society had not yet learned to accept and pave the way for people with disabling conditions.

Along the way on his own healing journey, Charlie came to understand an RX for healing that is far more powerful than medication and surgical procedures and restorative therapies – healing that goes deeper than cures or recovery. Charlie has had a lot of time to think about the difficult journey of healing; in this, his first book, he talks about the common threads that run through the kind of healing that is more than skin deep.

Charlie is the founder of Project 2 Heal, a non-profit organization that breeds and trains Labrador Retrievers to donate to children with special needs. He sees his own life-altering injuries as the catalyst that enables him to train these special dogs to be companions in and instruments for healing. What Charlie is often too humble to acknowledge is that he, too, was trained to heal by the accidents that once seemed like tragedies.

As you'll discover, Charlie no longer sees his childhood injuries as tragedies. He sees them as gifts.

The journey of healing has also been a journey of faith for Charlie. He makes no apologies for that. His intention in *7 Lessons for Healing the Hurt* is not to convert or to preach, but simply to tell the truth about healing as he has experienced it and, in doing so, inspire you in your own journey to heal whatever hurt you and your loved ones are experiencing.

Because Charlie knows that everybody hurts. He also knows, better than most people, that everybody can also heal.

- Peg Robarchek

The 7 Lessons for Healing the Hurt

On my personal journey to healing – physical, emotional and spiritual healing – I've learned the sometimes hard lessons about what it takes to heal. *7 Lessons for Healing the Hurt* explains how these hard lessons played out in my life.

The seven lessons are:

1. *Sometimes we get a cure; sometimes we heal.*
2. *Accepting the hurt isn't the same as giving up.*
3. *Healers love us back to health.*
4. *Believing is the best medicine.*
5. *There is purpose in the pain.*
6. *Give away the gifts.*
7. *Forgive everything.*

Thank you for the chance to share what I've learned with you. I hope some of the things I've experienced will have some healing effect on you, whenever and however there is pain and hurt in your life.

- Charlie Petrizzo

"He has told you, O man, what is good; And what does the LORD require of you, but to do justice, to love kindness, And to walk humbly with your God."
Micah 6:8 NAB

Hurt Changes Everything

Life will hurt. It will hurt us in ways that we think we can't survive and sometimes it will hurt so bad we might wish we hadn't survived. The things that hurt us will also hurt the people who love us the most. It hurts the innocent as well as the not-so-innocent. And when hurt happens, it changes everything.

Life Hurts:
Preparing for the Lessons

When I talk about what happened to me when I was a kid, I sometimes refer to "the accidents."

The accidents were defining moments in my life. They changed me physically and emotionally and they changed the very direction I expected my life to take. For a long time, I saw the accidents as the worst things that could have happened to me because they damaged my life in ways that felt tragic to me.

As we get older and hopefully wiser, the way we see things sometimes changes.

Looking back, I can see that the accidents didn't just change my life forever. They changed my entire family forever. The accidents hurt every one of us.

It's always like that. One person's hurt spreads, hurting everybody close to that person.

Of course, the opposite of that is true, too. One person's healing also heals everybody who comes in contact with that person.

When I was a few months shy of five years old, I was hit by a car. People who saw the accident said I flew through the air like a rag doll.

My family lived in a typical neighborhood in Staten Island, New York. The year was 1967. Kids played in front yards and made a lot of noise and there were always dogs and balls and skinned knees and even broken bones from time to time. Boys were expected to be rough-and-tumble and getting hurt was just part of playing hard.

I don't remember the accident, but it happened when I did something that kids everywhere do every day – I chased a ball into the street. Already, all I cared about was sports. I showed the promise of being a natural athlete, like my dad and my big brother. That promise came to an end when I chased that ball into the street.

I was visiting my godmother and her two children, who lived on a quiet one-way street on Staten Island. We had shared lunch and after lunch I begged my mother to go home with them that day; she wanted me to stay home. But I wanted to play and I wore her down.

We were playing wiffle ball, hitting the ball against the side of the garage. One of the balls went over my head and rolled down the driveway and into the street. I ran after the ball, darting into the street from behind a parked car.

A passing car hit me head-on. My head connected solidly with the car's bumper. I flew into the air and came down on the pavement.

When the police came, they found a little boy with a large flap of scalp and his left ear peeled away, his skull cracked wide open. Blood was everywhere. This was back in the day when few people came back from severe head trauma; you either died or you were permanently damaged and incapacitated. So a lot of people who were huddled around that day probably thought I was a goner.

The cops were worried, too. They didn't even wait for an ambulance, scooping me up, wrapping me in a blanket and racing me to the hospital.

"Will he make it?" my father asked the doctors when he and my mother got to the hospital.

The doctors hedged. "He has a 50-50 chance."

I was in a coma. My parents never left the hospital. After I'd been in a coma for several days, one of my mother's friends brought her a prayer card and a relic of Saint Jude – a piece of cloth from one of his garments.

"Carolyn, pray this novena to Saint Jude for nine days," mother's friend told her. "Saint Jude is the patron saint of hopeless causes. When he intercedes, sometimes there are miracles. Maybe he'll intercede for Charlie."

A miracle seemed to be exactly what I needed. So when her friend left, my mother prayed the novena to Saint Jude. She had just finished saying the prayer for the first time when she heard me crying and the nurse came running out of my room. "He's awake! He's talking!"

Even after I came out of the coma, the doctors told my parents not to expect me to walk again. My left side was paralyzed, not because of a spinal injury but because there had been extensive damage to my brain. But my parents refused to believe the doctors' prognosis.

Physical therapy wasn't sophisticated or readily available in those days, but after I came home my parents pushed me to do things for myself, believing that otherwise I would end up in a wheelchair for the rest of my life. Mother would pin me against the wall in an upright position and hold me there until my legs trembled, saying, "Stand up, Charlie! I know you can do it. Stand up."

Afterward, she would lock herself away in her bedroom or in the bathroom and cry. I couldn't have realized it then, but the physical therapy that seemed physically agonizing to me would have been even more agonizing, emotionally, for a mother who was already hurting for her little boy.

Eventually, thanks to my parents' determination and a lot of people's prayers, I did begin to walk and prove the doctors wrong.

I had also begun to learn what it's like for children whose physical or mental conditions leave them isolated from friends, from play, from the "normal" world that's still going on outside their bedroom windows.

The hurt looks different for every child and every family.

Some children, like me, have accidents that create long-term problems. Some children are born with disabling conditions like muscular dystrophy or Down Syndrome. Some children seem fine and then one day start showing signs of autism or symptoms of cancer.

The world is full of hurt.

Sometimes, that hurt is so bad that it can begin to consume our lives. It changes how we see the world and how we act with other people and even how we feel about ourselves. Personally, I believe that's especially true when the hurt starts in childhood.

Children who have to cope with illness or disability or trauma fight an uphill battle for a happy childhood. The playground or the public schoolyard can be tough places for children who are different, as my brother, Matty, and I found out. Matty is 16 months older than me and he was a straight-A student, one of those kids who never gets in trouble. But my father told me not long ago about at least one time when Matty heard about another kid who was mocking my scars and laid a beating on him.

So the hurt doesn't stop with the affected child. Chronic or life-threatening illness in a child threatens the whole family structure. The stress of parenting is multiplied and marriages are sometimes strained to the breaking point. Even brothers and sisters of a sick or injured or disabled child can be impacted in a profound way.

I know that not just because of my personal experience with Matty. I have a friend who has told me about her experience growing up with a sister who was stricken at the age of two with Spinal Muscular Atrophy (SMA). SMA is a degenerative disease that destroys muscles in the legs, arms, hands and, eventually, the lungs. My friend, Peg, tells me that her sister had three surgeries before the age of ten and wore heavy braces on her legs for years.

Here's what Peg told me about how this experience changed her entire outlook on the world.

"What I came to believe after my sister became ill was that the world is a dangerous place," Peg says. "I felt that no one – not our parents, not even God – can protect us from scary things that can never be reversed."

Peg was five years old when her sister began to lose her mobility. Peg remembers spending her entire childhood – and most of her adulthood – believing no one could protect her or her sister.

"It meant I was never really a child again," Peg told me.

Peg's experiences aren't exactly like everybody's experiences, of course. But the point is, hurt can spread through an entire family and through our entire lives. It touches everyone.

My brother Matty and I were born with a baseball glove in our hands. From the time I could walk I was holding a baseball and swinging a bat. Even at that young age, I felt like an athlete to the core. In the evenings, Dad would take us outside and throw balls to us so we could hit them, sometimes making me stand there until I could hit one. Dad was competitive and he instilled that in his boys at a very young age.

So just being able to walk after the accident didn't satisfy me.

I wanted to play ball again. I wanted to run and catch the ball and throw the ball and hit the ball. And I was still so young – barely six years old – that I had no idea how unlikely that was.

Probably because of the competitiveness my dad instilled and the natural ability I was born with, I did start playing ball again. First I played T-ball, like all the youngest kids, then moved on to Little League ball, where my Dad was a coach.

I played, but my balance and coordination and speed were off. I batted lefty and threw righty, which was the side most affected by my brain injury. So I had trouble throwing a ball with any degree of accuracy or strength. In six-inning games, I would only play three innings because the coach wanted to get better players on the field. I hated not being able to play the whole game.

In spite of my limitations, I was still a high-energy, determined little kid. For as long as I could remember, I'd wanted to play catcher. I probably liked the idea of putting on all the apparatus a catcher gets to wear. So every game, I would beg my dad to let me play catcher. But let's face it – a catcher has to be able to throw. And my dad never played favorites just because I was his son. In fact, he bent over backwards to make sure the other kids had their chance to play before he brought me in.

Then one day my dad's best friend and fellow coach, Al, said to him, "Why don't you just let the kid catch?"

Al and my dad were like brothers. Our families vacationed together, my brothers and I played with Al's kids and our mothers were close friends, too. So when Al spoke up, Dad listened.

In the fourth inning, after the other kids had played, my dad put me in as catcher. Sure enough, the other team hit the ball and the throw came to home plate. Maybe it was against all odds, but I caught the ball and tagged the other kid out.

Dad tells me that when I held the ball up, the smile on my face stretched from ear to ear.

Al smacked my dad on the shoulder, pointed at my grin and said, "That's why you let him catch."

By the time I was about 11 years old, I was one of the better players on a team that was bad. Extremely bad. Like the Bad News Bears bad. We lost every game we played that year. But I was able to play every position and after years of playing only half a game, I was allowed to play a full six innings. I was finally good enough to be chosen to play the full six innings.

All I wanted was to play ball. It was my dream year.

Then came the final year I was eligible to play Little League. The best players at that stage were drafted into what amounted to "the majors" in Little League and the ones who weren't stars stayed where they were to finish out their Little League career. I wanted to stay where I was, playing six innings, playing lots of positions and being one of the better players. Given my physical limitations, that's what would have happened to most kids.

In my case, it was complicated. My dad was a Little League coach – one of the best – and the majors wanted to keep him. He'd been one of their coaches when my older brother, Matty, played in the majors. The manager figured the best way to keep my dad as a coach would be to draft his son, even if his son would never be a star on a team of stars.

I knew what that would mean. It would mean very little playing time.

I told my dad in no uncertain terms that I wanted to stay where I'd been the previous season. I didn't want to be the player nobody respected and nobody really wanted. Even at that age, I understood that if they drafted me it would be because they wanted my dad, not me.

They drafted me.

I was as unhappy as I thought I would be. I didn't get much playing time, I wasn't as strong as the other players and I certainly got no special treatment from my dad, which I never expected.

I remember one Fourth of July weekend, when a lot of families always seemed to be out of town. That meant Little League baseball teams were sometimes short of players.

Because of Dad's coaching, we usually stayed around for the games. I remember one year when we only had ten boys still in town for the game and I thought, *Yes! This will be the day I play the whole six innings.*

I played the first three innings. At the top of the fourth inning, I put on my batting helmet. Dad came over to me; I could tell he was upset.

He said, "Take your helmet off. You're out of the game."

That day, I was the only kid who came out of the game, the only kid who wouldn't be playing the whole game. I cried and cried.

My dad says he and mom both agreed that if the accident had to happen to any of their three boys, I was the one who could handle it.

Apparently I was always energetic and determined and physically strong. I came back from the accident. Maybe that determination was tied to the fact that, for as long as I could remember, Dad had encouraged me to be competitive and athletic.

Had my injury never happened, I might have been the best kid in the field. I probably would have been like my brother, Matty, who played on all-star teams with the big kids.

Still, some natural talent and my sheer determination seemed destined to give me a chance at a pretty typical life. I could play ball, even if I wasn't the best. I had friends. I had beaten the odds those doctors had given my parents a few years earlier.

Until the second accident.

The summer I was sixteen, I had a job painting houses. My dad didn't want me to take the job.

"What's wrong with your paper route?" he said. "You're making plenty of money doing that."

I was sixteen and headstrong and I wanted to be doing what my friends were doing for the summer. Plus, I wanted to do physical work as a way of building strength and bulking up for football season. I took the job, which was supposed to be mostly clean-up and errands around construction sites. I ended up painting, too.

On July 16, 1979, we were just finishing up a job and noticed some spots of paint that needed to be cleaned off the shingles of the house.

It was almost noon, but we decided we could get the clean-up done before lunch. We had to move the 40-foot extension ladder and get it into position, which was awkward because of a nearby sidewalk and what I thought were telephone lines. As I gripped the extension ladder and moved it, it became unwieldy. The ladder tipped to one side and struck the nearby wires, which turned out to be not telephone lines, but power lines. The jolt of 36,000 volts of electricity knocked me to the ground.

The last thing I remember was an unbelievable sensation, almost like my eyeballs were being pulled out of my head.

Lesson 1:
Sometimes we get a cure; sometimes we heal.

Not everyone gets completely well, either physically or emotionally. But everyone, I believe, can experience healing. Getting cured means being as fit and healthy and whole as we were before the illness or injury. Healing is different. Healing can come even if we are never restored to wholeness or never become free of symptoms. Healing is a better place than we could ever get to without the illness. Healing is letting go of the hurt to make room for happiness.

Healing Happens

The dictionary says the word electrocution applies only to people who die. The only alternative is to say a person was shocked.

I don't think being hit by 36,000 volts can be compared to being shocked.

I was electrocuted on July 16, 1979.

I lived to tell it, but I shouldn't have. If you check Wikipedia, the on-line source of information, you can read that death from electrocution has occurred from as low as 32 volts. Shocks above 11,000 volts are "usually fatal," Wikipedia says. Shocks with voltages over 40,000 are "almost invariably fatal."

The 36,000 volts I experienced seared the metal ladder into my left side.

A kid who saw the accident said my body had an aura. I was green, purple and orange, he said, with a rainbow of fire around me.

Not long ago, during filming for the documentary *Charlie's Scars*, I met Buddy Fair. On the day I was electrocuted, Buddy was having lunch at the McDonald's across the street from the house where I was painting. Buddy's family sat down at the plate glass window that looked out at the four-lane street running between the restaurant and the house.

As we started to lift the ladder, Buddy said to his wife, "These guys don't look like they have much experience with ladders."

He saw the ladder start to sway, then fall into the electrical wires.

The day I met him, Buddy was wearing a bright orange Harley Davidson t-shirt. He pointed to the shirt and told me, "Your face and body were the color of this shirt."

Buddy reacted immediately. He jumped up from his lunch and darted out the door of the McDonald's to dash across the busy four-lane, completely oblivious to the fact that he could have been struck by a car and killed himself.

While we were taping, Buddy told me, "I could see your body, your side being cauterized, just melting into that metal ladder. I knew I needed to break the flow of electricity, otherwise this kid was going to die."

Buddy had played some intramural football and basically decided to tackle the ladder and me, again with total disregard for his own safety. Before he reached me, I fell into the street and the ladder fell behind me. I was facedown on the street.

As he approached, Buddy felt almost unbearable heat coming off my body. Trained in CPR, Buddy checked my vitals and realized I barely had a pulse.

He also realized that if he didn't cool off my body, I was a goner.

He looked around and spotted the water hose we were using to clean up the site, no more than ten feet away. Providentially, the water was running. Buddy grabbed the hose and began to pass the running water back and forth across my body, trying to bring the heat down. As he did so, he heard sirens coming our way. A fire truck skidded to a stop just inches from us, followed immediately by an ambulance.

"I've been at accident scenes before," Buddy told me. "But I've never seen them get someone into an ambulance so fast."

Later, I learned that the transformer blew at the school next door as a result of the accident, knocking out electricity for miles. If the transformer hadn't blown, the chances of my survival would have gone from nearly zero to less than zero.

And if Buddy Fair hadn't been eating lunch at the McDonald's, and reacted so quickly and with such presence of mind, I might've been dead anyway.

Sometimes, in the months that followed, I wasn't sure I would have chosen to survive if I'd known that the process of healing would meet every definition of hell.

Doctors said I was burned over 66% of my body, both second and third-degree burns. Internal organs and muscle tissue were also burned.

My feet were so badly burned that the doctors wanted to amputate both of them. My mother refused, challenging them to come up with a solution that would save my feet. As a compromise, they removed the severed tendon in my left foot. And instead of amputating the big toe area of my left foot, which is the balance point, doctors fused it into place at a 45-degree angle and inserted a pin. On my right foot, doctors removed the entire instep.

Although the external burns were agonizing in the months of my recovery, the worst of my injuries were internal.

First, a jolt of electricity that high is extremely hard on the heart.

During the filming of the documentary, one of the physicians at the hospital said the biggest concern at the time was the injuries to my left side. Although I was burned internally up to and around the stomach lining and intestines, the organs themselves weren't burned, which enabled them to intubate me for feeding. If that had not been possible, my survival would have been at much more serious risk than it already was.

Damaged muscles in my left torso did have to be removed, leaving extensive scar tissue and undermining the stability of the infrastructure that supports my body. Over time those internal injuries have had the most serious impact on me. From Hepatitis C to herniated disks and more, it has been the accident that keeps on giving.

Morphine was the drug of choice in those days for dealing with intense pain. The accident happened around noon and it was late that night before I came to in the hospital – this time in a burn unit at a hospital in New York City – for the second time in my life. Obviously disoriented, I still asked for my mother.

"I'm here, Charlie," she said.

I let myself sink back into the drug-induced fog. All I needed to know was that Mom was there.

I woke up later. I remember wondering what had happened to me. I looked down and all I could see was white netting and white cream. I remember thinking, *I broke my leg. It's not that bad.*

When my father came in, I said, "Dad, I love you."

To this day, Dad gets very emotional talking about that moment. At the time, they still didn't know if I was going to make it; the doctors were very honest with them.

"You never imagine," he said in the documentary, "having to see your child this way."

He and my mother could tell from looking at me, of course, that even if I survived, my life would never be the same, that my quality of life might be impacted even more by this accident than it had been by the first accident. Even the most superficial thing about the burns – scarring – would have tremendous impact on my life.

Scarring may seem minor compared to the other physical issues I faced after the near-electrocution. But being disfigured by scarring has a psychological impact that is hard to overcome – maybe especially for a 16-year-old. I was burned from my Achilles tendon up to my buttocks and from my belly button up to my trachea. I was devastated knowing that I would be disfigured with burn scars and by the surgery to remove muscle and tissue.

That's why you'll never find mirrors anywhere in a burn unit. Doctors don't want you to see yourself. They don't want you to lose hope.

27

Before this accident, I had been dating. But who would want to date someone who looked the way I would look for the rest of my life? I imagined a very bleak future for myself. I told my dad that no woman would ever want anything to do with someone who looked like me. I'll never forget the pain in his face when I said that. It was years later before I realized how devastating it is for parents to watch their children suffer through life-changing illness or injury.

Every night, when mom and dad left the hospital, I would cry. Besides the physical pain, I was being eaten up by self-pity and despair. Being different is bad when you're young. Being disfigured is **really** bad.

All I really wanted was to get my old life back. It took years before I could accept – **really** accept – that wasn't going to happen.

My body healed faster than my spirit.

The process for healing burns to the skin is called debriding. Basically it entails clearing away the dead skin so healing – sometimes in the form of severe scarring – can take place. I required 10 milligrams of morphine to get through it.

In those days, debriding took place in "the tank," which was like a giant bath tub. Every day I was taken to the tank and dipped in warm water. When the top layer of burned skin softened from the water, it was peeled off with a tweezer-like utensil to get to the very tender new skin underneath. It was agonizing.

Another part of the process I would compare to being hosed down. High-pressure spray was used to rip off more dead skin. Under every layer of dead skin was raw, highly sensitive tissue.

One area on my back was particularly painful; it had originally been diagnosed as a second-degree burn and later reclassified as a third-degree burn. On a day I remember very well, I started screaming when the burn was touched. More than once, I cried out, "I wish I was dead!"

A few years ago, I visited a burn center near the North Carolina town where I live. I had made the visit to speak with doctors and other hospital employees about donating trained dogs to juvenile burn victims. It was my first time to return to a burn unit and, almost thirty years after my time in a burn unit, I thought I was ready.

I was wrong.

What is Healing?

Healing is seeing the good that has resulted from your struggle.

Healing is overcoming the self-pity or despair.

Healing is knowing there's a gift in the worst that has happened to you – and knowing that the gift is yours to give away to others.

Healing is a place of joy where you accept all of it whether you understand it or not.

Healing is when other people see something in you that makes them want the kind of life you have – not the stuff or the money or any of those things, but the something inside you that they can't quite name.

Healing is finally letting go of the hurt.

I put on the sterile mask and entered the burn unit. It was very different being the one who was walking around looking instead of being the one in the bed. The smell of charred flesh brought back a flood of memories that were so painful I could almost feel the agony again. *I can't look at this*, I thought. *I'm not ready for this.*

Looking at people who were disfigured from their burns, I felt ill and almost fainted. Not because I was repulsed, but because it was the very first time I'd fully understood the magnitude of what had happened to me. As bad as their physical conditions were, I realized that I had been burned just as badly as any of them. I could remember the pain vividly.

Adding to my reaction was the full awareness, also for the first time, of the ordeal the accidents had

Healing Takes Patience

Some of the principles I use in training a dog also apply to healing.

One of the things people do wrong in training a dog is trying to rush it. Training videos show dogs making huge progress in one hour, with 15 minutes of commercials. So that's the way people think it will happen at home. But that's not the way it happens.

Dog training takes patience and so does healing.

When we're training a dog, if you have a dog that won't stay and at the end of a day the dog has learned to stay for ten seconds, that would be a big success. Enjoy it.

In the same way, when a child is sick or injured, we have to enjoy the little successes. We tend to look for the big enchilada, a miracle where a kid goes from being comatose to walking across the room in the last half-hour of a TV movie.

put my parents through. One hurting child hurts a lot of other people.

Looking into the eyes of the people in the burn unit was the hardest thing of all, seeing eyes that were full of fear or anger or – worse – that empty look of having given up.

As we walked through the burn center, I kept looking for my old enemy, the tank. I never saw it and finally asked, "Where's the tank?"

The person giving me the tour looked almost horrified. "Oh, no, we don't use the tank any more. That was like medieval torture!"

Today, the doctor told me, anyone undergoing debriding is placed under general anesthesia.

Not everyone gets well, either physically or emotionally. But everyone, I believe, can experience healing.

Healing and getting well are sometimes two different things. Getting well means being restored to complete physical health, being as fit or as whole as you were before the illness or injury, having no signs or symptoms of less than perfect health. Some people get well and they are blessed.

But healing is different. Healing can come even if we are never restored to wholeness or never become free of symptoms. Healing is a spiritual condition that everyone, every family can arrive at. Healing, in fact, is better than where you were before the sickness or the injury. It's a better place than you could ever get to without the illness.

Lesson 2:
Accepting the hurt isn't the same as giving up.

When the stakes are high enough – when we face something that could be life or death – most of us are fighters. It's against our nature to accept the fact that sometimes circumstances just won't bend to our will. Sometimes, we are as vulnerable as a two-day-old puppy, and just as helpless to change our circumstances. And that's not the same as giving up, although most of us have to go through that stage before we get to acceptance. Figuring out the difference between giving up and acceptance is when healing really gets hard.

Giving In Without Giving Up

I breed Labrador Retriever puppies. I'll talk about how that came about in Chapter Seven.

Right now, I want to tell you about Bean.

Bean was born in a litter of five beautiful pups. He was the color of a fox, which is one of the most unusual shades for a Lab. His color alone would make this pup a real stand-out, and he had a personality to match. I felt sure that Bean was going to be a very special dog.

How true that turned out to be.

Bean was one of the cutest pups in the litter, but he developed more slowly than his litter mates. By the time the other puppies were beginning to scamper around on their unsteady little legs, playing with each other and exploring their world, Bean still wasn't moving around very well. At feeding time, even the smaller pups in the litter were easily able to push Bean away. At a certain point, even the puppies' mother seemed to give up on Bean.

We realized he wasn't going to grow out of this problem when the puppies were switching from nursing to real food. After eating, Bean would regurgitate. Something was definitely wrong.

The vet who looks after our Labs told us the outlook wasn't good for Bean. Tests showed that our adorable Bean had a neurological condition called myasthenia gravis. It meant he might never walk.

For dogs, of course, that's the point at which vets sometimes encourage people to think about quality of life issues and whether it would be better to put an animal down.

For breeders like us, a diagnosis like that typically means it's time to cut your losses.

We just couldn't do that to Bean. And not just because he's so cute and cuddly and friendly and irresistible. That's all true. Our whole family was in love with Bean and losing him would have broken our hearts.

But what really made us willing to fight for the Bean was his combination of being a real fighter with his cheerful acceptance that he was different from his litter mates.

Bean didn't mope and whine and crawl under the sofa to hide. No, Bean was as rambunctious and

Parents Fighting Back

Now that I'm a parent, I can appreciate how helpless my parents must have felt after both of my accidents. They fought for me and challenged the doctors for me and encouraged me. But nothing they could do would restore me to perfect health. Nothing.

They were helpless to change that reality, no matter how hard they tried.

I see that same reaction in the parents I come in contact with through my Project 2 Heal foundation. They want to fight for their children.

If they fight for changes that can improve their children's lives, they open the door for emotional healing and wholeness for the family. If they fight to keep believing they can handle everything and that the hurt hasn't disrupted their families, they can block wholeness for the family.

happy as his litter mates. He was helpless to get better by himself, but he knew we were taking care of business and he trusted us to do whatever was right.

When I was four years old and lying in a coma and, even later when I was conscious but partially paralyzed, all I could do was trust my parents to take care of me. When I finally went home and faced the frustration of learning to pick up a spoon so I could eat by myself, all I could do was trust that my parents were right to let me learn how to do things for myself instead of just taking the easy way out and feeding me themselves. I didn't understand. All I could do was trust.

Ten years later, I was 16 and lying in a hospital again, incapacitated and damaged in ways that would never be healed physically. Once again I was helpless to change what had happened. But this time, I was miserable. I was in despair. I was depressed. Sometimes I was angry and sometimes I didn't want to keep going.

What made the difference?

When I was five, I had a fighting spirit. I believe that's one of the big reasons I survived. A fighting spirit is a good thing.

But at 16, I wasn't fighting as much as I was resisting. I did not want to be where I was. I did not want this to be my reality. I did not trust that someone I could depend on was in charge of the outcome. And because I didn't trust that I was being taken care of, I spent a lot of time asking angry questions like, *Why me? Why is God doing this to me?*

Because I wasn't getting any answers that made sense to me, sometimes I was still angry or depressed or self-pitying. Physically, over time, I healed as much as it was possible to. Emotionally and spiritually, I still had not healed because I believed that, unless I could be restored physically, I would never be whole again.

That turned out to be so wrong.

The way I was feeling back then wasn't fighting back. It wasn't even accepting reality, either. The way I felt then was resignation. It was giving up. I was refusing to accept that I could be happy any other way except the picture I had in my head. And I think I

Changing Lives

When we have a new litter of puppies, I marvel at their utter helplessness. Even their mother is helpless in so many ways. She can feed them and keep them from straying too far – at least for a while. But in the event something catastrophic happens, that Lab mother can't do anything. It's all up to me and even I can't control everything.

Yet my puppies have utter faith in their mothers and their mothers have utter faith in me. They know, when I hold their puppies in my arms, that I will not harm them and that I'll protect them just as fiercely as they will. When I'm getting to know those helpless little puppies, I find myself picking them up, looking them in the face and whispering, "I'm going to make you what you're here to become. And you're going to change somebody's life."

They don't hear me and they won't remember me saying that, any more than I remember the times when I was helpless and Mom or Dad – or maybe it was God – whispered in my ear, "I'm going to make you what you're here to become. And you're going to change somebody's life." But I believe that's exactly what happened.

felt that way because I didn't have a strong spiritual side to my life.

In my family, going to church was one of those Christmas-and-Easter kinds of things. So I was like the tree that gets hit by a big storm before its roots can take hold – destined to get blown over. I had a lot of fight in me, but I didn't have any of the faith that makes for the deepest kind of healing. I had Bean's fight, but not his cheerful acceptance.

I got better and stronger and I recovered, to a degree, from my physical injuries.

Inside, I still had a long way to go before I was healed.

You see, when life deals us a major challenge, we can be as helpless as a two-day-old puppy that can't begin to survive by itself. In those first weeks, a puppy has to depend completely on someone else – in most cases its mother – if it's going to make it. Under extraordinary circumstances, we're all in that position. We have to trust our support system, whether it's family or friends or doctors or our faith community or our neighbors.

And while we're accepting the fact that we're helpless without their help, we have to keep fighting. Like Bean.

The interesting thing about puppies is that the fear response doesn't kick in immediately when they're born. They go through a fear imprint period at about eight to ten weeks, then again at seven to eight months. But in the beginning, they're helpless and they simply accept it.

When puppies are born, they don't understand anything that's going on around them or anything that's happening to them. They can't see or hear or walk. The only thing standing between them and certain death is their mother and, sometimes, kind people who will protect them against things their mother can't fight, either.

But, unlike people when we get thrown into the unexpected and the unfamiliar, two-day-old puppies don't react with fear. They just seem to trust that somebody else is in charge and that someday their eyes will be open and it will all make sense.

When it comes to a life-changing illness or accident, we're unable to see where things are going to end up. We can't change our health by standing up to it and staring it down. We can't run from it and it's not afraid of our bark or our bite.

Being really okay when I'm most vulnerable means trusting that someone besides me is in charge. And it isn't enough to have doctors or parents or friends to turn my life over to. I need all of them, too. But I'll always be fighting to get things back the way I want them unless I believe someone is in charge who has a bigger plan in mind, who wants only the best for me and who will protect me in ways so powerful that I can't begin to understand them.

That's what it's like for puppies, I believe. They can't understand anything that's happening to them. So they just...trust.

It's too early to tell what Bean's life will look like over the long haul. His medication seems to be working and he's gaining strength and learning to struggle to his feet and stumble around a little. He's making progress. I watch him sometimes and remember what it was like learning to regain mobility – twice – with a body that had been changed completely. Other times, I watch Bean and think about the children I see who don't have some of the capabilities most of us take for granted and the pain that creates for those children and their families.

But whenever I'm with Bean, I remember that the best way for me to take care of him is to just let him struggle on his own to cross the room to his water bowl.

Bean knows he's being taken care of and he's okay with that. In fact, he always seems to be perfectly happy and full of enthusiasm, even when he can't do what other puppies take for granted.

That lesson was a lot harder for me to learn. I wanted to go back and be physically whole again. Today, I know there's a different plan for me.

Lesson 3:
Healers love us back to health.

Sometimes we expect our doctors to perform all the miracles. When we're little, we might expect our parents to kiss it and make it well. Healers are all around us. We have to keep our eyes open for everyone who shows up to love us back to health.

"There is no psychiatrist in the world like a puppy licking your face."
Ben Williams

Healing in the Circle of Love

The saving grace when I left the hospital after the near-electrocution was a dog named Toby.

For the second time in my life, I found myself feeling isolated from my friends. I felt so different on the outside that I couldn't imagine ever being just a regular guy again. I had faced death – a second time – and I had come back a different person. There was a chasm between me and the friends who had continued doing what teenagers were doing in the early 1980s – going to school, resisting homework, competing in sports and cruising for chicks.

Emotionally I wasn't 16 any more. Physically, I wasn't regular Charlie any more.

So where did I turn to feel better about myself? To animals.

To boost my sense that I could still be competitive, I turned to horses. I thought as long as I could sit on that horse, I was still an athlete, as good as the next guy. All I had to do was hold onto the reins and sit the horse. Speed and agility were still required, but they were up to the animal; my role was to guide.

But for love and acceptance and a sense that I belonged, I turned to my dog.

This wasn't the first time I had been profoundly affected by a dog. My first eye-opening experience with a dog had come when I was about 10 years old on a trip to Atlanta with my family, where my dad was being interviewed for a job. The family we stayed with had a beautiful black Labrador Retriever named Molly. I fell in love with Molly. I fell in love with the breed. Molly, like most Labs, was friendly and gentle and enthusiastically playful and unconditionally loving. Most dogs have those traits, but Labs have them in abundance.

I loved that dog so much that when we returned home I wouldn't leave my parents alone until they let me get a dog of my own, a mixed breed that probably

Fear Interrupts the Circle of Love

Labs aren't the only source of love for a child or a family in physical or emotional pain. Love is all around them.

Sometimes, people or families with special needs withdraw and won't accept the love that is crucial to healing their hurt. Sometimes people don't feel comfortable giving their whole hearts to those with special needs.

Those fears interrupt the circle of love. When that happens, the hurt keeps on.

All of us need others – friends, neighbors, family, dogs, sometimes even kind strangers – to love us back to health.

Whenever others offer us help, what they're really offering is their love. They bring meals, and love comes with it. They give us a shoulder to cry on, and love comes with it. They cut our grass or do the carpooling for a week or offer to watch the kids so we can rest and recuperate – whatever they offer when we're hurting, what they're really offering is love.

Some of us don't like to accept help. We like being self-sufficient. We think we can take care of ourselves. That keeps us in our pain instead of opening the door to healing our hurt.

Service is love in action and we all need it sometime. When we accept the help people offer, we're setting in motion a circle of love that heals everyone it touches.

had a little bit of Lab in him. That dog, Toby, became my best and most loyal friend. And when I returned from the hospital, that dog became a healer in my life.

Feeling different on the outside is always painful, but never more so than in the teen years. In my mind, the questions kept repeating over and over in my head: *Why me? Why did these terrible things have to happen to me? What did I do to deserve a fate like this?*

I can see now that those questions were being answered by my friendship with Toby.

My love for Toby was a major hint as to what I was put here to do, and how I was to find meaning in everything that had happened to me. Coming home to a dog who loved me unconditionally, no matter what I looked like and no matter what I'd been through, eventually healed some of the worst of the hurt. And it planted the seeds for the most important work of my life.

So there I was – a young man with his whole future ahead of him, feeling like his best years were surely behind him. Sixteen years old and wearing a hairpiece to hide the scar tissue on my skull, I tried to pull my life together.

Inside, though, I still spent a lot of time asking, "Why me?"

Because I wasn't getting any answers that made sense to me when I asked the "why me" question, sometimes I was still angry or depressed or self-pitying. Physically I had healed as much as I was going to. Emotionally and spiritually, I still had not healed.

Scarred, physically challenged, often in pain, I was determined to make the best of a tough break. I threw myself into finishing school and getting into college. But part of me was holding onto the old me and the old dreams I'd had for my life. In college, I studied sports marketing, thinking if I couldn't be an athlete maybe I could take my passion for sports into the business end of sports.

Still, fear got in my way, mostly fear of being humiliated and fear of being rejected by girls.

I remember a fraternity social that sort of epitomized how I felt about myself and the fears I lived with. At this social, the partying had progressed to throwing people into the pool for fun. Not only did my hairpiece look pretty pathetic, it felt like straw, it was itchy and sweaty where it was taped to my head, and being thrown into a pool would have been disastrous. I could imagine myself, wet clothes clinging to a torso that no longer had a perfectly normal shape with a pathetic hairpiece floating beside me. If that happened, I felt certain, my social life would be over.

I found a chair, got as far away from the fun as possible and spent the rest of the evening terrified of being found out.

I continued for a long time to be very cautious when I was around anybody except family, especially in mixed company. In fact, the main reason I joined a fraternity was because it increased my comfort level to have a frat house full of friends who didn't judge me. I almost started to feel "normal."

Then I met a young woman who seemed to be able to look past my physical problems. We decided to get married. We planned a wedding. I looked into the future and saw myself with a wife and children I could teach to play ball and the whole white-picket-fence lifestyle that any kid growing up in the 1960s wanted just a little bit.

Six days before we walked down the aisle, the woman I was supposed to marry walked away.

After she broke it off, I looked into the future again and it looked pretty bleak. Who could blame her? Who would have me, with the challenges I faced? Who would want me, looking the way I looked?

I was broken-hearted and miserable. Worse than that, I became a little more bitter. I built up a little more emotional scar tissue around my heart.

When I finished college, I worked for a friend's travel agency, where I sometimes chaperoned trips. One weekend, my friend asked me to chaperone a bus trip for a bunch of kids from a Catholic school. I had always loved kids, so I thought it would be fun. And it was fun. It was fun to be with the kids and it was fun to be helping out.

The principal liked me and the way I interacted with the children. After the trip she approached me. "Have you ever thought about being a teacher? You don't need a teaching degree for Catholic school."

I didn't know that, but when she asked, working with children sounded a lot more satisfying than being in the travel business. I accepted her offer.

Shortly after that, I ran into a girl I knew slightly from my college days. She'd been three years behind me and was a member of my fraternity's sister sorority. In college, I thought she was pretty, but a real Miss Goody Two-Shoes. It was just as well I wasn't interested in her because she thought I was a loud mouth – well, she didn't *think* it, she *knew* it.

By the time we met again, I was still boisterous and loud and she was still quiet and gentle. But by this time, I had matured enough to recognize that this pretty woman with the beautiful eyes was somebody special.

Her name was Sandy. On July 9, 1989, Sandy and I got married. I just knew that this woman's love was going to turn my life around.

That turned out to be true. It just took longer than I expected and it didn't happen exactly the way I expected.

The love of Labrador Retrievers is a big part of my life today. Of course, Labs aren't the only source of love for a child or a family in physical or emotional pain. Love is all around them.

Sometimes, people or families with special needs withdraw and won't accept the love that is crucial to healing their hurt. Sometimes people don't feel comfortable giving their whole hearts to those with special needs.

Those fears interrupt the circle of love. When that happens, the hurt keeps on.

All of us need others – friends, neighbors, family, dogs, sometimes even kind strangers – to love us back to health.

Whenever others offer us help, what they're really offering is their love. They bring meals, and love comes with it. They give us a shoulder to cry on, and love comes with it. They cut our grass or do the carpooling for a week or offer to watch the kids so we can rest and recuperate – whatever they offer when we're hurting, what they're really offering is love.

Some of us don't like to accept help. We like being self-sufficient. We think we can take care of ourselves. That keeps us in our pain instead of opening the door to healing our hurt.

Service is love in action and we all need it sometime. When we accept the help people offer, we're setting in motion a circle of love that heals everyone it touches.

I know what can happen when dogs come together with hurting children, and you never know when you're going to cross paths with hurting children and their families.

One of the things I enjoy most is taking Labs out into the community. Nothing brings out the joy in people like a dog. Children and adults, everybody wants to pet and hug and get doggie kisses from our Labs. Just seeing it happen time after time brings me a joy I can't describe.

Plus it's an ice-breaker for me and I don't worry quite so much that children will have a bad reaction to my scarring when I have a Lab on the end of a leash. So the Labs and I go to festivals and parks and for walks in the "downtown" of the small town where my family lives. We even go to industry trade shows and farmers markets and outdoor concerts – anywhere people congregate.

My most memorable encounter was at a trade show a few years ago. I had a young puppy with me who was already experienced at meeting people in public places.

That particular day, a little girl about eight years old came by with her parents. She was in a wheelchair; she had severe physical disabilities that kept her from walking or moving her arms.

When she saw the Lab puppy, I saw the light in her eyes.

"Would you like to hold him?" I asked her.

There was no hesitation in that little girl's face. So I lifted the puppy into her lap and helped her put her arms around him. The puppy, of course, curled up on her lap and licked her hand and wagged its tail and let her know that he was as delighted to see her as she was to see him.

No one who was there that morning had dry eyes when that little girl looked up, a huge smile on her face, and said, "Daddy! Look at me! I'm holding a puppy!"

That is the healing power of simple love, given with no strings attached.

It's true, that little girl wasn't physically healed when that puppy sat in her lap and rubbed its wet nose on her arm and made her squeal with delight. But in that moment, any hurt she might have carried disappeared. The hurt because she wasn't like other children or because she was isolated from the fun of childhood because she required a wheelchair for mobility – that hurt no longer existed for those few moments.

That's what the Project 2 Heal foundation is all about – breeding and training Labrador Retrievers to be companions for children with special needs. Others may train dogs to heel; we train ours to be part of the healing process. We know it works. Our puppies become part of a healing circle that allows us to love each other back to health.

Here's what that circle looks like:

A Labrador Retriever, who has been raised gently and with love, gives love to a little girl in a wheelchair by sitting in her lap because she's too weak to hold it in her arms.

That Lab's love gets transformed into that little girl's smile and the joy in her voice and everyone around her knows she's experiencing a healing moment.

That little girl's smile gives a degree of healing to everyone who witnesses it, especially her parents, who take dozens of photographs.

A little bit of healing and hope is transferred to everyone who looks at the photographs that were taken that day.

People who witnessed that love in action tell the story to people who weren't there and the circle of love continues.

That circle of love heals everyone it touches.

Even – maybe especially – the guy who bred and trained the dog.

Dogs and Love

Experts in canine behavior will tell you that dogs don't love us.

They will tell you that dogs are opportunists who learn how to get their wants and needs met by doing what people want them to do. If they fetch, they get a treat. If they heel, they get affection instead of scolding. If they lick our faces or curl up at our feet, they get food and a warm place to sleep.

They don't do these things to please us, canine behavior specialists say. Dogs become attached to us because we meet their needs and provide for their wants.

In other words, dogs learn how to get their needs met. They do it by exhibiting behaviors we like. In the process they become attached to us because we do meet their needs. It's that simple and that basic.

Dogs learn to do things that feel like love and devotion to humans. Maybe that's not love in the way that saints or psychologists define love. The saints, for example, define love as willing the good of another. In other words, love is consciously and intentionally doing things that create good in the lives of others, and doing so with no expectation of receiving any reward for it.

Based on that definition, dogs don't love in the truest, most spiritual sense. Of course, a lot of humans don't, either.

I also know from my own experience that, whether it's because of attachment or opportunism, dogs make us *feel* loved. And that is healing. For that to happen, dogs must be brought up and taught how to interact with people using one guiding principle: Love follows love.

And healing follows love.

Lesson 4:
Believing is the best medicine.

Healing when we're really hurting means trusting that someone is in charge who has a bigger plan in mind, who wants only the best for us and who will protect us in ways so powerful that we can't begin to understand them.

> *"When tragedy strikes, we enter a crisis of faith. We either move toward God or away from God."*
> *Dr. Bob Kelleman*

Testing Our Faith

Sandy, I thought, would make my life perfect. And her big heart and her faith and her love for me were certainly factors in my healing.

But I had to find out, one more time, that no human power could give me everything I needed to face life's big hurts. That would be the biggest lesson of all.

Once Sandy and I married, we started thinking about starting a family and preparing for the future. And with the idea of having a family to support, I started thinking the way a lot of men think: How could I make sure my family would be financially secure? How could I make enough money to do that? Teaching in a Catholic school, obviously, was not going to get us where I assumed we needed to be financially.

So during the boom years of the economy, I turned to business and started a career in the financial industry.

I did well – my life was definitely getting turned around – and ended up with a high-level position with one of the country's largest financial institutions in the Wall Street of the South, Charlotte, NC.

Sandy and I had everything – a big house, nice cars, clothes, electronics. Money was abundant and money was the number one ingredient in the American Dream. Right?

The problem was, we still didn't have a family.

We wanted children to share all this abundance. But it didn't happen. We tried to be patient. Surely the God Sandy believed in so devoutly wouldn't do this to us – to *me*, after all I'd been through. Over the years, we watched as friends who got married much later than we did started families. And we were still childless. It was eating at Sandy and it hurt me to see her hurting.

With a sense of dread, I finally decided to see a doctor. He confirmed what I had been fearing: because of all the internal damage from the electrical burns, it was highly unlikely that I could father a child.

I was devastated. Despite everything I'd been through, I don't think anything had been as hard to take as learning that I would not be able to give Sandy a child. I wanted children, too; I love children. But to disappoint Sandy...it was the final straw in a life of bitter disappointments.

Clearly, God didn't love me. Why should I love and serve a God who would treat me this way?

I turned my back on God.

I grew up in a Catholic home, doing the pretty typical Catholic thing for that time and place – we went through spurts where we went to Mass regularly but for the most part we went on Christmas and Easter. The rest of the time, my dad, my brothers and I were much more interested in football, hockey, basketball and baseball than we were in sitting through what I considered a long, boring Mass.

I attended a Catholic university, but I can't say that did much to instill faith in me, any more than the half-hearted religion I'd practiced when I was a kid.

When I was hired to teach middle school history for the Catholic school, the message of faith started to drip on me. I had to lead the children in prayer in the morning. Every Wednesday, we had to attend Mass. I didn't really understand much of what I was being exposed to, but I found myself starting to fall in love with the rituals and the message I seemed to be hearing and reading about.

Then I met Sandy.

Sandy was a rock of faith. Not an evangelizing Catholic, but someone who practiced her faith regularly. I saw how she treated people and what she did for people because of her beautiful heart. And I thought that must be what it meant to be a person of faith.

Of course, when God gave me the great gift of a woman like Sandy in my life, I didn't ask, "Why me?" I suppose deep inside I thought I must deserve a gift like her, after all I'd been through.

I was grateful and I was willing to let God into my life. But my faith wasn't mature enough to understand the magnitude of this gift and how it would be part of changing my life.

Finding out that Sandy and I couldn't have children felt like I'd been smacked down by a God who didn't care about me. I cried. I let God know how unhappy and disappointed and angry I was.

Are you kidding? What next? Why me? I would demand of God. I did not have the patience of Job. I wanted to argue with God, and I did. *What are you doing to me, God? After all that I've been through, now I can't even give my wife a child?*

Sandy's strong faith had been a big influence in my life. But when this happened, I was at such an early stage of my own faith that I wasn't ready to be tested. I stepped away from God, despite Sandy's patient attempts to get me to see that God might have a plan in what was happening to us.

My response to her was, "You're telling me there's a God that's done this to me?"

Her response to me was that I needed to find out why this rock had been put in front of me.

I stopped going to church. We started the adoption process. I told myself maybe this was God's plan for us. If so, I didn't like the plan. But I would do it for Sandy.

Thankfully, Sandy continued to be faithful. She went to Mass. She prayed. She didn't give up hope. She always believed.

We decided to adopt and learned that the adoption process could be as frustrating as the process of trying to get pregnant when the odds were against you. It involved assessments and intrusion into our personal lives that we never imagined. But we stuck with it and we were approved and I suppose we expected to become parents pretty quickly.

Two years into the process, we were still waiting.

I worked on Wall Street at the time. One day in June, 1995, Sandy called me at work. She was crying so hard I couldn't understand what she was saying. "Calm down," I told her. "Talk to me slowly."

She took a deep breath and said, "We got a baby!"

"What?" Maybe I still wasn't understanding her.

"We got a baby!"

I started screaming. Even in the big, noisy room where I worked, my shouts grabbed people's attention. "We got a baby! We got a baby!"

Although I could tell she was still crying, I heard Sandy ask, "Don't you want to know what it is?"

"What is it?"

"A girl. It's a girl."

By this time my boss had come over to listen in. He started gesturing toward the door. "Go! Go!"

Wearing my suit and my wingtips, lugging a briefcase, I went flying out of 1 Wall Street into the humid June day and ran for my car.

My dad helped make flight arrangements so we could fly into West Palm Beach, Florida, that evening.

The next morning we drove to the adoption agency. Before we could see our baby girl, paperwork had to be completed. Thankfully, the paperwork went quickly. Then a woman walked through the door with a bundle in her arms, our 21-day-old baby girl.

Sandy was shaking when the baby was put into her arms. I was trying to capture everything on video but doing more crying than filming.

We named our daughter Melissa.

Here was this beautiful, precious little baby, a gift from God. I thought, okay, God, I'll come back to church and praise you.

I went, but I never really examined my faith and I never really saw that I, too, was being offered a chance to live my faith the way Sandy did.

A year and a half later, Sandy and I were watching the Eagles play the Cowboys late on Monday night football when the phone rang. It was a man from work; he and his wife were just starting the process for a private adoption.

They hadn't yet completed all the requirements, but his wife had been placing ads to look for women trying to place their babies. They had heard from a woman who was a week away from giving birth when the couple who had intended to adopt her baby backed out.

With no guarantees, we flew to Arizona to see if we could become parents a second time.

The birth mother okayed us to be present for the birth, so we spent a week carrying around the pager that would signal us that she was in labor. We arrived in time to be there for the final minutes of our second daughter's birth.

About a week after that first call, on October 10, 1996, we had Kristen in our arms.

Now, I thought, we're a typical American family. Now, I thought, maybe God is going to leave me alone and the good life everybody else enjoys is going to start for me.

By the time the girls were school age, I wasn't going to church any more. I wanted to stay home, watch a Panthers football game on TV – any excuse not to go listen to things I only half believed. Yet I was giving Melissa a hard time when she resisted going to church.

"Why do I have to go?" she asked her mother one Sunday morning. "Daddy doesn't go."

That was a sign to me. I told Sandy to give me ten minutes and I would be ready to go to church with them. From that point, I went to church to be an example for my daughters. But believe? I just didn't. Not the way Sandy did.

In 2004, I left my job in the financial arena, walking away from a high six-figure income. I didn't yet know what I wanted to do with the rest of my life, but I knew that finding ways to put more money in the pockets of people whose pockets were already full felt meaningless.

On the surface, I seemed to have everything a man could want, but something was missing. Disillusioned and a little angry at some of the things that had happened to me during my time in the corporate world, I walked away and immediately started to wonder, *Now what am I going to do with myself?*

Physically, I still suffered, as well, and that contributed to my depression that had been building since I left my job.

Even after my physical injuries healed, my body has never been the same. Because the muscles in my upper left torso were removed, the imbalance in my body would mean that the remaining muscles would have to work overtime to compensate. The imbalance also caused my spine to twist. As a result, 30 years after the accident, I have a number of herniated disks in my neck and lower spine.

False Beliefs

When it comes to healing, we have to believe we can heal. Sometimes there's a cure and sometimes there isn't. But healing is always a possibility. When I was hit by a car a few months before I turned five years old, the doctors said I'd never walk again. My parents didn't believe that prognosis, so I didn't either. If I had believed the doctors' pessimism instead of my parents' hope, I might not be walking around today.

When I almost died from electrocution, I believed I'd never have the kind of happy life kids expect when they're growing up. I believed no one would ever love me. I believed I'd never find anything in life I wanted as much as I wanted to be around sports.

All those were false beliefs.

When I found out my injuries would keep me from fathering a child, I believed God must have it in for me and that I had somehow been shut out of finding the happiness everybody else gets to experience.

More false beliefs.

For a long time, I made myself a lot more miserable than I needed to be because I refused to believe – didn't have *faith* – that God was bigger than my problems.

Imagine building a house on a foundation that's cracked on one side. The house might look okay, but because the foundation is cracked, other parts of the structure have to take up the slack to hold the house together and keep it upright. After years of wear and tear, that lack of a solid and balanced foundation will cause problems. Over time, even the well-constructed parts of the building will start to break down due to the stress of over-compensation.

That's what had happened to my body.

Because of the pain, there were many nights when I couldn't sleep. My body had mended as much as it was able to, but I was still walking around with physical disadvantages that will always be with me. The doctors had predicted that I would have physical problems by middle age. They were right.

Emotionally, I felt weighed down, too. My mother, who cared for me all those years, was struggling with chronic leukemia. No longer a bastion of strength, she became a feeble shadow of her former self as the leukemia ravaged her body.

After all she had done for me when I was recovering from my accidents, I wasn't able to be at her side during her illness – all because I had chosen money and business over family.

Shortly after I left work, Sandy's father was diagnosed with lung cancer. He died about a month later. My mom's illness worsened until she lost her battle.

The two deaths threw me into an emotional tailspin.

My mother, I often felt, had saved my life by believing in me and in my ability to heal when even the doctors didn't believe. And now she was gone. I fell into a familiar depression, that old "why me?" place.

Sometime after these events, I remembered an idea that had come to me when I was just a kid, after our trip to Atlanta when I met Molly, the beautiful black Labrador Retriever. I told my father one day, "I'm going to breed dogs like Molly when I grow up."

My faith is very important in my life. It has made me who I am. I can honestly say that hasn't always been the case. I was my own god and leading my life. I thought nobody knew better than me. I had a plan and I was going to follow it.

Now, knowing my life was at a turning point, I began to research the field, looking at it through my businessman lens. Where were the business opportunities? How does a guy make money with dogs? I started studying animal behavior and training on-line through the Animal Behavior College. Then I earned an advanced diploma in canine fitness and nutrition through the Companion Animal Sciences Institute. I couldn't get enough of it. But I was still looking for the financial angle.

While doing research on the internet, I found what I was looking for: a franchise opportunity that used dogs for drug detection in schools.

Perfect, I thought. It paired my love for dogs with a concept that seemed to have real value. Schools that wanted to deter drug use and dealing among students could bring in a private company with dogs specially trained to detect drugs. Unlike the police, a private company didn't need probable cause to do such a search. Also unlike law enforcement, a private company could allow the school to handle contraband on a case-by-case basis; in some of these instances, this would prevent a criminal record being established for a student who made one bad decision. Needless to say, I liked the idea of creating second chances for troubled kids.

I went out to Houston, Texas, for training. I thought I was buying a franchise, but God had other plans.

In Houston, the hotel where I stayed for the week-long training at Interquest Detection Canines turned out to be across the street from a Catholic church. I was an early riser, but the training didn't start until 10 every morning. The church had Mass every morning at 8:30. I thought maybe I'd go, just for something to do that first day.

I went the second day, too. It was better than sitting alone in a hotel room.

On the third day, the priest asked me if I would read for the Mass.

Here I was, a life-long Catholic and I didn't even know how to read for Mass. But it made me feel really good to be part of the liturgy, so I made it a point to be there the next day and the next day. I realized that Mass was a nice way to start the day.

As it turned out, I tried for more than a year to find a client after I completed my training. Few schools, I discovered, were willing to risk the liability that came with bringing in a dog owned by a private company to conduct a drug search despite the benefits. Had my time in Houston – not to mention the money I'd spent – been a complete waste?

After Houston, I didn't have any success with my business venture. But something fruitful had clearly come out of that trip.

When I came home, I kept going to Mass on weekdays. A group of ladies at the church got me involved in praying the Liturgy of the Hours every morning. I started studying how the service had evolved and why we did the things we did in church. One day I was asked to teach a class. Then I was approached by a nun about a teenaged boy on a troubled path who needed someone to sponsor him for the sacrament of Confirmation. Seeing as how the request came from a nun, how could I say no?

What had started as a slow drip years earlier, when I taught in a Catholic school, began to snowball.

I'm not sure exactly when I realized that I had become a person who believes instead of a person who doesn't believe. But I do know this: Once I really believed, everything was in place for me to heal completely.

Learning to Trust Life

The epiphany for me came when I realized I wouldn't be raising Labs to detect drugs or even to sell for high dollar to people interested in top-of-the-line show dogs. I would be raising Labs as skilled companion dogs and providing them to hurting children.

That meant a very rigorous and different kind of training for these puppies.

Training for our skilled companion dogs starts with early neurological stimulation. Early neurological stimulation begins when puppies are two days old and ends at 16 days. Especially in the beginning we do a bunch of things that may not seem to be teaching the puppies much that has any value. But the training that comes in those first weeks may be the most important training we do.

One of the very first things we do is take a cotton swab and tickle the pads of those puppies' tiny little paws. They've never felt anything like that, of course. So it startles them a little at first. But because they're so young and they trust that everything is happening exactly the way it's supposed to be happening, they quickly adjust. In a few days, those cotton swabs are just one of the many sensory perceptions that are part of their brand new lives.

Over time, we begin to blow gently on their faces. We cradle them in a supine position. We lay them on cold towels. We make sure they are handled by as many as a hundred different people by the time they're ready to be placed in a home, so they are accustomed to different smells and sounds and touches.

The point of the exercise with the cotton swabs and the rest of the sensory stimulation is to prepare them to experience the unexpected and novel stimulus without over-reaction.

We're teaching them to trust life – and the people who are protecting them – even when life throws them a curve ball that they didn't expect and don't understand. That is part of the training they'll need to be good companions for children with special needs, who can be just as unpredictable as most things are in life.

When you come right down to it, learning to accept with grace the things we don't expect and don't understand – even when life throws us curve balls – is a big first step in healing the hurt that comes with those curve balls. Like our puppies, we just have to believe we're in good hands.

Charlie's Album

Charlie and his big brother,
Matty

Charlie, center, and his brothers Matty and Cono

The Petrizzos: Cono, Carolyn, Matty, Charlie
and young Cono

Sandy and Charlie

The Wedding Party

Carolyn and Cono

Charlie and his brothers

Melissa and Kristen

Charlie's mom, Carolyn Petrizzo

Lesson 5:
There is purpose in the pain.

When we connect the pain in our lives with our God-given talents and passions, we have found the purpose in our pain. Once again, everything changes – this time, it changes for the better.

> *"I have found the paradox that if I love until it hurts,*
> *then there is no hurt, but only more love."*
> *Mother Teresa*

Surviving to Serve

Medical science said I should have been dead twice.

Then why am I here?

I think anyone who has survived a near-fatal illness or accident asks questions like that? Why was I saved? Why did I survive when so many don't? What does it mean that I'm still alive and relatively able-bodied?

And, of course, that finally leads to the question we all ask at some point in our lives: What am I supposed to be doing with this precious life I've been given?

I apparently thought the answer, if you judge from my actions for so many years, was to make as much money as I could by helping other people make as much money as they could. I had become a creation of the culture corporate America has built – consumerism.

That just doesn't add up for me any more.

In college, I studied sports marketing. My passion, I believed, was sports and if I couldn't be an athlete, I could at least spend my life around sports. It wasn't long before my love for children trumped that goal and I ended up teaching at a Catholic school. But when Sandy and I married, financial security became a driving motivation for me.

I had become fascinated with the concept of annuities and that became my passion and my career. I started as a telephone representative for Prudential, then became the director of sales and marketing for one of the largest bank distributors of annuities in America.

While I was with the bank, I invented an insurance product that allowed people to invest in various sectors of the stock market and reduce their tax liability; the underlying product chassis was the annuity. We partnered with an insurance company and the S&P 500 on the product and initially it sold like hotcakes. Eventually the marketability of the product was hampered by international constraints on exchanging some foreign currencies for American dollars as well as limitations some nations placed on the amount of money that could be sent out of their countries. The product was pulled.

When I was in that invention/creation mode, I loved what I was doing. But once that came to an end, I started to discover that there was something hollow in my work in the financial industry. I realized that my perspective on money and materialism was changing dramatically. I had to get out. I had to do something else with my life.

We're a consumer nation, but when you start serving others, it puts things in a different perspective. And once you start living the paradigm of serving versus being served, everything gets turned on its head. What becomes important is taking the talents and the passions you've been given and using them in service to others.

I thought about breeding Labrador Retrievers. I learned the best techniques for training dogs. I learned canine nutrition. I spent hours researching careers and ended up buying the drug-detection franchise. I spent about a year trying to build that franchise, but in the end it didn't work. I was training and working with dogs, but I didn't get to care for and nurture the puppies.

It was only when my faith led me to a different understanding of service that I finally realized how I was supposed to be putting this passion for animals to work.

Remember the first time I fell in love with a dog, when I was about 10 years old? My dad visited Atlanta and the man he visited had a beautiful black Lab named Molly. My whole week was about Molly. I told my dad right then that one day I was going to have a Lab like Molly. It was like my purpose in life had been pointed out to me at the age of 10 or 11, like God saying to me, "All right, kid, there you go."

I guess I just wasn't paying attention; it took me about 30 years to get it.

When I stopped thinking so much about how to make money from this passion and more about how to use it to be of service, my deeper purpose in life became clear to me: *I could combine my love of animals with everything I'd learned from my experiences as a seriously injured child.*

I would breed dogs. And not just any dogs. I would breed Labrador Retrievers with a pedigree carefully selected for the traits required for the best service dogs. I would train the best pups in every litter as service dogs and companions. Then I would give them to children I understand – wounded, hurting children. Ultimately, in addition to the puppies I gave directly to children, I also donated pups to skilled companion training programs in other parts of the country that trained puppies for the same purpose.

I made a decision to follow not a career, but a purpose: Project 2 Heal was born.

Sandy and I found three acres in the countryside near Charlotte. We bought that land and began to transform it into a facility for carrying out the work we felt called to do. We launched a non-profit organization.

All the pieces of my life fell into place like a jigsaw puzzle.

Life is full of pain. But when I was able to connect the pain in my life with my God-given talents and passions, I could see the purpose in the pain. I know now that there is always purpose in the pain, as long as I am willing to use what I've experienced to serve others.

One of the amazing things I've come to understand is that by living out this purpose, everyone wins. I experience the joy and the love that grow out of serving others. Children and families who are hurting find comfort or stress-relief and a little bit of healing.

Even the Labs win.

In breeding Labs and evaluating litters of puppies to select the ones that are best suited to be companions, I've recognized that it isn't just people who are given special talents and passions. So are animals. Through Project 2 Heal, I have the opportunity to train every dog to develop its own individual traits so it can be happiest doing what it does the best.

Or, as my mentor, Sally Bell, says, "We don't want mindless tail-waggers. We want a dog that has a reason to be happy."

Some puppies are instinctive trackers; this makes them perfect companions for children who tend to wander away. Some have a calming presence, which makes them wonderful for children who tend to have

Serving the Common Good

There's a social doctrine to my Catholic faith, which says that if you own private property it should serve the common good in some way.

This belief is behind my idea of creating a dog park where people can come to play with their own dogs or with one of our companion dogs. I see families that are dealing with chronic health issues or permanent injuries walking away from that day with an unbelievable smile and a memorable break from the hard challenges of their everyday lives.

I am not the owner of the land; I am the steward of it. My faith tells me to use it to benefit others.

tantrums or get highly agitated when they are stressed. We've brought dogs in to interact with autistic children who tend to become very agitated and the dog's presence almost immediately begins to calm them down. Other puppies have so much patience with children that nothing a rambunctious child does will upset them. When we send dogs out to interact with children who have trouble reading, children overwhelmingly respond to the unconditional acceptance and love of the dog – they readily read to a dog because they know the dog isn't judging them if they read slowly or mispronounce a word. Another dog may be so adaptive and intuitive that it can give a family exactly what is needed in a situation that can change from minute to minute.

Even Labs who aren't suited to be skilled companion dogs have a purpose to fulfill. Some are simply so loving and loyal that they will be valuable members of a family that just wants a pet to love and be loved by. One way or another, it's clear that love heals, maybe even in cases where nobody realizes there's hurt.

Thanks to the work I do, I have the privilege of helping all the Project 2 Heal puppies develop their unique abilities and become the very best they can be. With the unique gifts I've been given, I can be part of helping these puppies live out *their* purpose, too.

Because I can see the purpose in the pain, things that once felt like my bad luck don't seem like bad luck at all any more. Those accidents that almost destroyed my life became part of my calling. If it weren't for all the pain I experienced as a little boy, I wouldn't have it in my heart to do what I can to heal the hurt for other little kids who are hurting today.

I live my life in a different way now. A decade ago, my life was about having nice things and getting very comfortable in the world.

Now I have a purpose.

I can tell you this with absolute certainty: Now that my life is about serving others instead of getting something for myself, I am happier than I have ever been.

Can people still see signs of my injuries? Do I still feel physical pain on a regular basis? Yes, to both those questions.

In spite of that, would I say I'm healed? You bet I am.

Lesson 6:
Give away the gifts.

Realizing there is a gift for us in life's most hurtful experiences eases some of the pain. But healing is more than just easing our own hurt. True healing comes when we experience the total joy of easing someone else's hurt. When we do that, we've multiplied the healing in a hurting world.

> *"Our prayers for others flow more easily than those for ourselves. This shows we are made to live by charity."*
> C.S.Lewis

Giving Away Our Gifts

Not long ago I received a call about a man who was heading to Iraq; before he left, this solder wanted to find a dog for his niece, a blond-haired, blue-eyed little girl who is autistic.

This soldier, his sister and his niece came to the Project 2 Heal facility to see how the child reacted when she met one of the Labs.

I spent some time getting to know these family members. The little girl would mumble, but wouldn't speak. We all went outside to meet the Labs; I watched the little girl for signs of fear. When she seemed to be comfortable with the dog, I asked if she wanted to see the dog chase a ball.

Before long, the little girl was jumping and clapping and squealing. Most importantly, she was speaking, saying words like "ball" and "please" and "thank you."

Watching from the patio, this mother began to cry as she watched her little girl having as much fun as any other kid let loose in a field with a dog and a ball.

Off and on for years, I didn't believe I had anything to live for. I kept thinking about everything that had been taken away from me. I was so focused on everything I *couldn't* do that it never occurred to me to live in gratitude for all the things I *can* do.

In my case, I see how every misfortune in my life was leading me closer and closer to the day when I had accumulated some really valuable gifts and could finally use those gifts the way they were intended to be used – I could give them away to others.

Who doesn't love receiving gifts at Christmas and birthdays? Especially when we're children, it's so exciting to rip into a package and see something shiny and new that now belongs to us.

I don't know about you, but as I grew up I figured out that giving a gift was actually a lot more fun than receiving gifts. It was fun to buy a gift and imagine someone enjoying it. It can be fun wrapping a gift and imagine watching the excitement of a kid ripping into the package. It can be fun even years later when we see people wearing or using or enjoying a gift we gave them.

> What I finally understand – what led to my philosophy whether I'm training dogs or transacting with another person – is that the God I believe in is an all-good, all-loving God who created us to do His will. So what I do must be all-good and all-loving.

So as happy as I am when I've discovered and embraced my gifts, I'm happiest now that I've figured out how to give my gifts away to make the world a better place.

When I talk about giving our gifts away, that doesn't mean we can't make a living using our gifts and doing what we love. It just means that if making money is our *first* priority, it's going to be harder to realize the full potential of our gifts.

When I first decided to breed and train Labs, I thought of it as a new career that I hoped would be as lucrative as my career in the financial industry. The plan for using my gift didn't really begin to take off until I recognized it as my gift to the world, a form of service that was uniquely mine.

I'm a Catholic and the priests tell me that as a believer I'm called to practice acts of mercy on behalf of other people. There are Corporal Works of Mercy and Spiritual Works of Mercy. The Corporal Works of Mercy are things like feeding the hungry and giving shelter to the homeless and visiting the sick. We're all responsible for doing things like that.

Spiritual Works of Mercy are not so concrete and we don't all have the particular gifts to do some of them, like counseling the doubtful or instructing the uninformed. But the priests at my church tell me that I can use my gifts to comfort the afflicted. I am uniquely gifted to do that because I know what it is to be afflicted and need comfort, and because I know how to equip Labrador Retrievers to be instruments of comfort.

Here are some of the ways I give away the gifts I've been given.

Project 2 Heal provides puppies for inmates to train for the Indiana Canine Assistance Network.

We work with local schools for children with behavioral issues.

We visit senior communities, where the Labs are always welcome visitors. Our goal is to encourage active seniors to volunteer with us to interact with the puppies. It's good for the puppies and it's good for the seniors.

And, of course, we match puppies with children who have special needs.

These dogs are the source of the service I am here to give to the world. I am here to love the dogs and give them the opportunity to develop their unique ability. Every day when I wake up, I think, "God is giving me these dogs to nurture and love today, so they will be ready to give to someone else."

Every day, people reject the gifts that come with their adversity.

God comes at us with open arms, full of gifts like love and family and health and intelligence and opportunities to serve and special talent that makes the world a more beautiful or joyful place for all of us. And sometimes all we can see is pain or separation or rejection or loss or scarcity or limitation or aggravation.

To heal, we have to be able to say "yes" to the gifts God brings us. Sometimes I've said, "Yes, but…" That's not going to work. I have to say "yes" even when the gifts don't come in the package I think they should come in. I have to say "yes" even when the gifts come with pain or loss or disfigurement or disability or disappointment.

But how can we get there from that place of brokenness?

"Yes, thank you" is a start.

If I can stop saying "Yes, but..." and say "Yes, thank you" things begin to change. The way I feel about things starts to change. The way I react to things starts to change. Finally, the way I see things in my life starts to change.

Gratitude is a life changer, especially when life seems to be at its worst.

But what can we be thankful for when life has kicked us and we're down? Start with the most obvious things. Say thanks for still being around to breathe in and out. Say thanks for the people who love you no matter what. Say thanks for sunshine out the window or the rain that's keeping the grass green. Say thanks for a roof over your head. Say thanks for breakfast or lunch or dinner, even if it's just a can of beans. If you can't walk, say thanks for being able to move your arms. If you're too weak to pick up your kids, say thanks for two good eyes to watch them play. If you can't pay the mortgage, say thanks for the abundance of being able to pay bus fare to look for work.

There is always something you can say thanks for. Always.

And the more I say thanks, the more I see in my life to be grateful for. The more I say thanks for the gifts I have, the more gifts show up in my life.

Lesson 7:
Forgive everything.

Bitterness, anger and hatred are not compatible with healing. Forgiveness sets us free from anything with the power to hurt us. Forgiveness restores us to that place before there was hurt.

Forgiving Everything

I get reminded all the time that I still have a long way to go on my spiritual journey. And healing of any kind is basically a spiritual journey, isn't it? Our bodies were created to heal, but our spiritual walk has a lot to do with how successfully we will heal.

In so many ways, I'm still a baby in this process of spiritual healing. I've been healing from physical injuries most of my life, even long after my accidents as my body continues to adjust and compensate. So I've been at the physical healing a long time.

Spiritually, there are times when I feel like I can barely walk.

One of my most powerful lessons in healing came in the fall of 2010, when I travelled with a group of men from my church on a mission trip to Jamaica.

We were in Jamaica to serve with the Missionaries of the Poor, a monastic order founded by Father Richard Ho Lung. Father Ho Lung has been compared to Mother Teresa for his dedication to working with the poor in Jamaica, Haiti, India, the Philippines, Uganda and Kenya. Missionaries of the Poor is a small order, but under Father Ho Lung's leadership it has grown from four to 550 brothers across the world.

It was a little intimidating to think about working with and maybe learning from a man like Father Ho Lung.

Before visiting Jamaica, I thought I understood poverty. I'd seen poor neighborhoods in my town, within eyesight of the towers where some of our nation's biggest banks were headquartered. In the shadow of those towers, homeless people caught my eye as I entered and exited freeways. I had seen Angel Trees and other collection points in the lobbies of businesses, set up so disadvantaged families could celebrate holidays or have school supplies. So I knew about poverty.

It turns out I didn't know poverty. Not the kind of grinding, dehumanizing poverty I saw first-hand in Jamaica, which is an island where people come from all over the world to luxury resorts where they can soak in the sun, eat rich food, shop till they drop and enjoy cocktails topped with little paper umbrellas. But beyond the boundaries of those resorts is poverty.

Working with the Missionaries of the Poor to serve this kind of poverty was a life-changing experience for me.

Something else was happening for me during that trip, something that I didn't realize was transforming me until almost a year later: I saw first-hand the healing power of forgiveness.

One of the first things I saw when my group reached the monastery in Jamaica was a photo of two young novitiates. Below the photo were their dates of birth and the date they died. Even before I heard the story, it was hard to take my eyes off the photo. They were so young. Too young to have died, I thought.

In Jamaica, just as in many major cities, gangs are a problem. Where gangs exist violence can erupt.

The two young novitiates whose photo hung in the monastery had been murdered when a bullet entered the kitchen where they were cleaning up after a party to celebrate a senior brother's departure to a mission in Africa. The bullet went straight through the first novitiate and entered the second, killing them both.

After investigation, the authorities learned who had committed the murders. Father Ho Lung had the power to prosecute them.

But Father Ho Lung had lived in the land of the poor for so long that he had something I believed I could never have had under those circumstances — compassion. Me, I would have been ready to drop the cyanide pellet. Having been electrocuted myself, I still felt that some crimes just deserved that kind of consequence. Compassion was for people who had a lot more faith than I seemed to have.

How compassionate were Father Ho Lung and the brothers?

As part of the work of the Missionaries of the Poor, the monks and other volunteers built houses for families that otherwise lived in shacks made of sheets of cardboard or tin, often sleeping four or six or eight people in a space the size of a walk-in closet in a typical suburban home in my city.

When it came time to build a house following a hurricane, the first house the Missionaries of the Poor built was for the man who murdered their two young novitiates.

That stopped me dead in my tracks.

I could not have done that. That is the faith of a saint, someone who has the courage to walk the walk of the apostles centuries ago.

I had made the trip to Jamaica to work for a week as caregiver for orphan children who were severely disabled. The priests with the Missionaries of the Poor did that, as well, making sure compassionate treatment was given to children who would otherwise be society's cast-offs. This was not the sweet work of rocking beautiful little babies and singing lullabies until they fell asleep. We spent a week handling the personal needs of children living in the harshest of circumstances. It was physically demanding and it was mentally hard to handle. The brothers told us to do what we could and when we could do no more, to take a break. The people we had come to serve would be waiting for us when we returned.

Looking back at that mission trip, I now understand that the trip and the task we had signed up for was just the vehicle for my next lesson in healing.

In the process of writing this book, I was approached by two talented young filmmakers who wanted to make a documentary about Project 2 Heal.

Beth Jenkins Sowell and Randy Davis with Episode XI Studio wanted to do more than make a few short videos for YouTube or for the Project 2 Heal website. Randy and Beth wanted to go all out to tell the story in a documentary.

One of the things they wanted to do was interview others who had been around during the accidents and at different stages of healing. We flew back to New Jersey to interview people about my accidents – a doctor who treated me, the hero who crossed four lanes of traffic to cool my body with a water hose, even my dad.

We also flew out to Indiana to tape interviews at the women's prison where I donated puppies for a training program coordinated by Dr. Sally Irvin. The inmates trained the puppies and the puppies were then given to those in need of a service dog.

During the trip, I was struck by the caliber of the women inmates who were part of the program. I saw the way they handled the dogs and how they interacted with each other.

I knew the prison was maximum security, but I couldn't imagine the women I'd met being involved in serious offenses.

After the trip to Indiana, I Googled the prison.

What came up in the Google search shook me to the core.

On January 11, 1992, a 12-year-old girl, Shanda Sharer, was kidnapped, tortured, sodomized, stabbed and set fire before she died 10 hours after her ordeal began.

Four teenage girls were convicted of the crime. The acknowledged mastermind of the crime was Melinda Loveless, who was 16 years old at the time.

Melinda Loveless was one of the inmates participating in the dog training program.

I was sickened and enraged. This woman – this *monster* – was part of my mission of healing! She held and cuddled my puppies. They licked her face and wiggled in her lap and made her laugh. And maybe, just maybe, the fact that she was involved in the project would make it easier for her to be paroled one day. After all, one of the other three girls who had participated in this heinous crime had already been paroled after participating in the dog program.

I felt violated. I was ready to shut down the program, pull the plug on the documentary. This, surely, was not part of God's plan.

I'm not going into a lot of details here. What happened after that is central to Beth and Randy's documentary, *Charlie's Scars.* I hope you'll watch it.

But briefly, Beth, Randy and I flew back out to Indiana Women's Prison. I needed to sit down face to face with Melinda Loveless. I needed to know that my puppies weren't serving the selfish motives of a brutal and heartless killer.

Truthfully, I was looking for the smallest excuse to back away from the program for the inmates. I did not want to forgive this ogre.

During the interview, I came down hard on Melinda Loveless.

Now in her early 30s, Melinda had been in prison about half of her life. She talked about having been saved. She talked about being remorseful. I wasn't one hundred percent convinced. Didn't people like her make claims like this all the time, hoping to be released?

I also spoke to Shanda's mother, Jacque Vaught, who warned me not to be duped by a murderer's crocodile tears.

Soul-searching can be painful. And I was agonizing over the revelations about Melinda Loveless and my role in her life and what God expected me to do with this bizarre twist of circumstances.

Another Child, Another Violent Death

When he was fourteen years old, my father lost his little brother. Matthew was just three days away from his tenth birthday when another kid put a shotgun to his chest and killed him. Matthew was declared dead at the scene.

Matthew and the other boy, who was 12 years old, had a run-in earlier in the day. The 12-year-old said it was an accident. Was it? The system ended up saying it was an accident. One of the boys who was there told my father later that it was no accident.

My father, Cono, carries that around with him to this day. He will not even discuss the option of forgiving the boy who was responsible for the death of his little brother. I have a little brother, too, and I can't say I would be able to do any differently under the same circumstances.

But I also know that hanging onto his anger must be a heavy burden for my father, and a shadow on his heart.

The day after interviewing Melinda, I was in the airport in Indiana waiting for my flight back to North Carolina. My anger over what Melinda had done was eating away at me. I didn't know how to be free of this anger that was turning more and more bitter the longer I dwelt on it.

Then I looked up and saw a priest walking down the terminal to his gate. I jumped out of my seat and ran after him.

The priest was a campus chaplain for Purdue University, heading to Charlotte for a wedding. After chasing him down, I told him the whole story of what I was struggling with, hoping, I suppose, for some kind of special dispensation to condemn Melinda Loveless in my own mind.

But, oh, no, it wasn't going to be that easy.

Essentially this priest told me that if I would pray for Melinda every day, it would become harder and harder to harbor ill feelings for her. He told me I would begin to see her as a human being who had made a choice to commit a horrific act, and that Project 2 Heal might finally be offering her a way to heal herself and offer healing to Jacque Vaught as well.

So in the weeks after that, I tried to start doing what the priest in the airport had suggested. I also found the story of Father Richard Ho Lung and the Missionaries of the Poor coming back to me. I remembered the way they forgave the man who murdered their two young novitiates.

But I'm no saint! I told myself. *I can't be like them!*

As if my mental anguish weren't enough to deal with, my own memories of the excruciating pain associated with being burned came back to me in full force.

Also, my conversations with Shanda's mother, Jacque Vaught, put me right in my own parents' shoes. For the first time, I think I fully understood the depth of my parents' pain.

Like a lot of men from his generation, my dad is a man of few words, especially when it comes to his feelings. The most emotion I've seen him display about my accidents was during filming for **Charlie's Scars**, when he got choked up talking about the first time I spoke to him after the electrocution. But after talking with Jackie Vaught and hearing the pain in her voice, I found myself wondering where he stood on the issue of forgiveness.

On the day I was electrocuted, the guy who had hired me pulled up on his way to the job and asked if my dad had a wooden ladder we could use for the job. The wooden ladder we had was too short, so he said the aluminum ladder would have to do. If we'd hit the electrical wires with a wooden ladder, the outcome that day would have been very different.

"Do you forgive him?" I asked my dad during the filming.

"Nope," he said without a minute of hesitation. "He knew right there that giving you that ladder was putting you in jeopardy. Yet he allowed you to work with it. He knew from that day on that he'd better stay out of my way."

Dad turned to me then and said, "Have you forgiven him?"

The question surprised me a little. "I don't think I ever thought of blaming him," I said. "I guess I was too focused on things like how I was going to live with this new look."

I understand where my father and Shanda's mother are coming from. Forgiving is hard. I remember conversations I've had with friends about people facing the death penalty for horrific crimes. I've actually said, "Let me pull the lever. I won't have any trouble being the one who does it."

> "Forgiveness is the remission of sins. For it is by this that what has been lost, and was found, is saved from being lost again."
>
> **Saint Augustine**

But the problem with not forgiving is that it eats away at the one who harbors the anger, not the one it's directed at. When Jesus tells us to forgive, he isn't saying we have to go out and throw a party for the person who hurt or wronged us. He's just saying we're supposed to forgive, the same way we hope others will forgive us.

About a month after the first interviews, I flew back to Indiana with Beth and Randy. We had scheduled another interview with Melinda; she was going to have to convince me that her remorse was genuine before I could continue. Then, if I was convinced, we would take that video to Jacque Vaught.

If Jacque agreed, Project 2 Heal would continue to provide puppies for the inmate program and Melinda Loveless would be allowed to train a puppy to honor the memory of her victim, Shanda Sharer. If Melinda couldn't convince me or if Jacque remained unyielding, the program was in jeopardy.

The morning of the interviews, I was up long before daybreak. I went for a drive, to pray and wrestle with the conflicting emotions I was experiencing. The devil was having a field day with me as I went back and forth between wanting to forgive and being unsure I had enough faith and courage to ask a mother to forgive the unforgivable. Already I had been the subject of a lot of nasty comments from people on Facebook who wanted to remain on the side of hatred. It wasn't easy, especially when I had so many conflicting feelings myself.

As I drove, I did what I often do when I'm in a spiritual battle. I called my wife.

Sandy calmed me down and helped me remember that whatever happened in the day ahead was not about Charlie. This was God's plan. I didn't have to know what the end was going to look like. I just had to show up and let God talk through me.

In the end, Project 2 Heal won out. Which is to say, God won. I'm not saying everybody forgave everybody that day, but little miracles happened and I think those were miracles of healing that I got to be part of.

Sometimes, long before I ever heard of Shanda Sharer or Melinda Loveless, when a litter of puppies was born and it came time to send them to Indiana to be trained, I would ask myself why in the world I was working with people who were incarcerated halfway across the country when there were prisons near my home in North Carolina. It didn't seem to make much sense.

Today I understand that I was supposed to be sitting there with Melinda Loveless, watching her break down and sob uncontrollably when I told her that the mother of her victim had given permission for her to train puppies in honor of a beautiful 12-year-old girl who died a hellish death at her hands. I understand that I was supposed to be there with Jacque Vaught when she hugged me and whispered in my ear, "I think it's what Shanda would have wanted."

And I think I was supposed to be there to learn that we all need forgiving and we all need to forgive if we expect to be free to heal completely.

Conclusion:
Celebrating All the Gifts

I like to say that I want to heal the world, one puppy at a time.

Some people might think that's overstating what one person can do, raising a few litters of puppies every year, looking for the handful of children those puppies can help.

That wouldn't be the first time in my life I've been told something is impossible. I've been given miracles to achieve the impossible before.

Who's to say there won't be more miracles?

One day, Project 2 Heal won't have three acres, it will have a minimum of 30 acres. It will be the home to a state-of-the-art breeding and training facility that will enable us to give the gift of companion dogs to many more hurting children than we can serve today.

I see an amusement park where dogs and their families can come together to play and explore in beautiful natural surroundings.

I even see people who have found purpose in learning the training techniques that produce the best companion dogs – a part of my dream that is already coming true through a partnership with the Indiana Department of Corrections. Through that partnership incarcerated women whose lives have been broken by crime or poverty or addiction learn the trade of dog training.

Their lives are transformed and the majority of them never return to prison once they are released.

That's how it works. Everybody is transformed when they are touched by the gift that grew out of my accidents.

What looked like a tragedy to me is actually an act of mercy for all of us. It started with me, but because I was willing to heal, there's a long line of healing – from Sandy to our children to the children we serve to the parents who love those children and all the way to the broken people who are finding their own healing by training these dogs to be a healing presence for others.

If that's not a chain of miracles, I guess I don't understand the definition of miracle.

Two things that enabled me to heal physically were a loving family that offered support second to none, and my competitive nature as an athlete, which gave me the desire to overcome any obstacles put in my way.

But true healing goes deeper than physical healing. I had to discover things in me that I didn't even know existed before I could experience true healing. I had to find a passion for something outside myself. I had to develop a strong desire to help people, using my passion and my own personal experiences. And I had to gain faith, a defining faith.

Those pieces of the puzzle weren't in place when I was 16. And they didn't come to me all at once in a burning-bush experience. I spent years struggling with self-pity and depression, going back to the "why me?" question every time life dealt me a hard blow.

But over time, everything that happened — especially the hard blows – worked together to change me radically from the inside out. The result is that today, 30 years after my second "accident," I am not just different on the outside from the person I was 30 years ago. I am completely different on the inside.

Our bodies were created to heal. With time and good doctors and the body's own natural ability to heal, an awful lot of physical injuries get better. My injuries did get better, even if they didn't get well. And I don't care how much we might want to give credit to doctors and medicine and surgery, ultimately it's the body itself that does the healing. So, to my thinking, healing is a miracle.

What's harder, sometimes, is getting over the trauma of injuries or fatal illnesses or chronic conditions.

Our lives are disrupted, and we don't forget that very easily. Our bodies may never be the same and don't allow us to forget. We learn what it means to be afraid and helpless and we can't just forget that because the immediate danger is over; now we know how vulnerable we – and all our loved ones – are. Sometimes our dreams for ourselves or our children or our families are destroyed and we just can't forget how far our lives are from what we hoped they would be.

But if anything is more resilient than the human body, it is the human spirit.

Although I continued to ask "Why me?" more than once over the years, eventually I awakened to the miracle of true healing. I was given a healing of the spirit that allows me to live in gratitude instead of bitterness or self-pity. I see myself as a lucky man, a blessed man.

Celebrating is easy when we're cured of whatever ails us. It's a little bit harder when we know we may never be cured, we may never be without scars or we may never again be completely whole.

That's why it's so important to focus not on being cured, but on healing.

Healing comes about through a series of little everyday miracles. If we're focused on the miracle cure to whatever is wrong with us, we might miss all the small things that add up to healing. Part of the healing process is to look for today's small successes and celebrate them.

My Inspiration

My work is inspired by the legendary story of Saint Roch, a French nobleman whose life was changed by the love of a dog.

The man who became Saint Roch was born near the border of France around the late 13th Century, the son of a nobleman. Even his birth has been called a miracle because his mother had been barren until she prayed to the Virgin Mary. When the child was born, he had a birthmark in the shape of a red cross on his chest.

When he was 20 years old, this young nobleman's parents died and he inherited many worldly goods, which he gave to the poor. Then he embarked on a pilgrimage to Rome. He arrived in Italy during an epidemic of the plague and began to tend the sick. It is said that he caused many miraculous cures with his prayers, the sign of the cross and the touch of his hand. Finally he fell ill himself and went to a hut in the woods to recover or die. He would have perished except for a dog that brought him bread and licked his sores, healing them.

When he returned to France, he was arrested as a spy and thrown into prison, where he died five years later without revealing his name. After his death, the townspeople recognized his birthmark.

Legend has it that after his death, an angel laid under his head a tablet with a gold inscription that said anyone who calls on Saint Roch will not be hurt by any pestilence.

The story of St. Roch has a great deal of meaning to me for several reasons. First, he gave his life to the cause of helping people who were critically ill, and I'd like to follow in those footsteps. In the process, Saint Roch became ill himself, so I identify with someone who became an outcast because of his own sickness. I was never an outcast, but any child with a chronic health problem can tell you that they always feel outside the circle of "normal" children.

And finally, Saint Roch experienced healing thanks to a loyal and compassionate dog. In fact, icons of Saint Roch often show him with a dog carrying a loaf of bread in its mouth.

The Project 2 Heal Story

When the Project 2 Heal dream comes to full fruition, here's what it will look like:

- A **30-plus acre facility** with a breeding facility, kennel and a dog park
- 15-20 puppies in training continuously, representing a line of puppies that they are as close as possible to **perfect as skilled companion dogs**; those whose individual personalities are not suited for service work will be sold to support the cause
- Highly **trained volunteer staffing** to assist with every facet of socializing, training and caring for the puppies and adult dogs
- A carefully constructed **process for matching dogs** with the children they will companion
- A Disney for dog lovers: a **destination dog park** with indoor and outdoor activities where families can experience dog-friendly amusement and where families without dogs can enjoy the companionship of specially trained dogs
- **Partnerships with various organizations**, including local colleges, rescue missions, correctional facilities and non-profits serving special needs communities
- **Partnerships with corporations** in the pet care industry that want to provide financial support for providing companion dogs to special needs children

- **Compassionate dog training** for pet lovers who want their animal friends to learn in an environment of unconditional love instead of under a model of punishment and domination, with proceeds supporting the Project 2 Heal cause.

No one at Project 2 Heal will have a job, but rather a vocation, a true calling.

About Charlie Petrizzo

Charlie Petrizzo is the founder of Project 2 Heal, a non-profit organization that breeds, trains and provides Labrador Retrievers at no charge to children who face challenges such as autism, Down Syndrome, burns or other injuries and chronic illnesses.

Before launching Project 2 Heal, Charlie was in the financial industry.

Originally from New York, Charlie now lives in Waxhaw, NC, outside Charlotte, with his wife, Sandy, and their two children, Melissa and Kristen.

Charlie's Scars

If you've enjoyed *7 Lessons for Healing the Hurt*, you don't want to miss the documentary film about Charlie Petrizzo's journey, ***Charlie's Scars***. Visit the website at www.charliesscars.com.

Made in the USA
Charleston, SC
18 March 2015